Eleven:

Things We Never Said

by

Carlos Harleaux

ELEVEN: THINGS WE NEVER SAID

Copyright ©2018 by Carlos Harleaux

Published by 7th Sign Publishing

(www.PeauxeticExpressions.com)

All rights reserved. No part of this book may be reproduced or transmitted in any form or by any means without written permission from the author/and or publisher.

ISBN 978-0-692-16351-1

Book Cover Design and Illustrations by AC Phlyers

Photography by Renato Rimach

Introduction

I pour much of my personal feelings and thoughts into my writing. However, there are some things I like to keep privately to myself. All my books come from an inspirational place. I must be led to write them and then led again to share them with the world. I still have tons of poems that have never been published, because I haven't been directed to release them.

This is a book I never wanted to write. My ex-wife and I got a divorce earlier this year. We were together for over eleven years (including dating and marriage). Whew! Just to put it in perspective, we both spent nearly all our 20s together. In a sense, we were kids that grew into adulthood together. There were more rough times than good at the end of the marriage, but everything happens for a reason. I would be lying if I said we didn't have our share of laughs, love, smiles and affection for each other. At least that's how I like to think of it.

The amazing part about our relationship is I can count on one hand the number of times that we argued. Some people may say that's a blessing. Looking back, it was a small crack in our foundation that eventually became an enormous fault line. One of our biggest arguments was right before we got married. We were both heated about our personal viewpoints. Now, it seems like the silliest thing to argue about. Honestly, it was minute in the grand scheme of things.

There were several things that we didn't say (or say strongly enough) in year one, two, three, four or five, that made it harder to communicate the longer we stayed together. By the time we were more upfront with each other, the damage had already been done and sadly, it was irreversible. Nonetheless, I still love her and appreciate the good times. There are three sides to every story. Both parties involved have their own versions of truth and what really happened is somewhere within the murky waters in the middle.

There is no bad guy (or girl) here. This is merely a collection of feelings as they happened, during the divorce process. My hope is that anyone reading this book can relate to it and use it to inspire them to work it out in their relationships, avoid some pitfalls before entering a relationship or face the music following a painful breakup.

Here we go....

Table Of Contents

Binge Watching	8
Picket Fences	10
Empowered	11
*Be Kind. Please Rewind	12
Hate You If I Could	14
Mr. Responsibility	15
Freezing Rain	16
*Oh, The Rain Is Here	18
Jealous Of Your Pillow	19
Wrapped Up	20
Maybe So	21
There She Goes	22
*When Crazy Stops Making Sense	24
Backpedal	25
Remember	26
Let's Do It Again	27
I'd Rather Be	28
*Stress Is A Hell Of A Drug	31
Losing Ground	34
How Does It Taste?	36
On This Day	38
Color Me Pink	40
Boy Toy	41
Chandelier	42
*Stay Woke	44
Worth A Thousand Words	46
And The Award Goes To	48

Limbo	49
Delusions Of The Third	50
*Turning In The Keys	52
Heartburn	54
Choked Up	55
Here's Looking At You	56
Distraction	57
*The Definition	60
Where Is My Receipt?	61
Syrup	62
All The Things You Hate	64
Hearts Bleed	66
*What Really Happened?	69
Freckles	70
Walking Egg Shell	71
Now. Then. See You Later.	72
Try Love At Your Own Risk	74
*Going Through Withdrawals	77
How Are You?	78
Skin To Skin	80
Labor Of Love	82
*Forgiving Us	83
Same Ole Love	85
Insomniac	87
The Trouble With Being Myself	90
*It's A Different World Now	92
Yellow Grass	94
Relationship Goals	95
Bring Back The Shadows	97

*Water With No Lemons	98
Grim Reaper	99
October 31st	101
Lights On, Lights Off	102
*No Price Tag For Peace	105
I Don't Know	106
Happy Birthday	108
I Don't Want To	109
*Good To See You	110
Shrimp and Grits	112
Let It Flood	115
*The Dam Must Break	116
Running Nowhere Fast	118
Pep Talk	120
Tomorrow Will Come	122
Never Again	123
Day In December	125
Know This	126
*Out of Order	128
^Excerpt from *When the Cookie Crumbles*	130

*denotes original essays

Binge Watching

I have replayed the entire series
Of our love
To the point of ad nauseam
Until my iris started to dim the light
Allowed to travel
Through to my retina
I feel like a failed pupil
Looking at the debris from
All the calamity
I am unable to mend
This is us
Filtering through the grey anatomy
Of love
Learning how to
Get away with a broken heart
In the end
No more good times
But I'm lucky for the time
That we had 'em
You were my beautiful golden girl
I was charmed by a single smile
Now it's back to living single
And oh, we're just friends now
Maybe I'll catch you sometime
On the fifth floor
How did we burn to such a
Scandalous existence?
Law and order
Signing papers
Now I'm insecure about
Everything you ever said

About everything we ever did
My walls are up and
So is my fear factor for
Slipping my feet in
The shoes of love again
I won't walk in them
I will leave them where they stand
There's no full house here
Just me, myself and I
Plus the remote
On to the next episode

Picket Fences

I never really wanted or needed
A perfect love without blemish
I just wanted something real and fun
In this life
Free and elevating me, with no limits
I never yearned for perfection
Just a sign that we were traveling
In the same direction
I'm guessing it was all a lie
From something held back deep inside
I don't believe in fairy tales
But I pray you find yours in a
Whimsical horse and carriage
Because, truly that's what you deserve
Honestly, I just wasn't the one to ride
In like a knight in shining armor and give it to you
Bitter much?
You better believe it
How we got here?
I can't fully conceive it
I never really cared about those
Pointy picket fences
They all look the same anyway
They all eventually give way
They all fall to scratch us in the eye
They all creak, break and split
In the middle of the night
Just give me something
To hold it all together

Empowered

I respect your honesty
As humbling as it may be
That is beside the point of
Reflection
I'm glad your introspection
Led you to this very moment
Otherwise we'd be living a lie right?
I respect the punches blown and
Really have no choice but to roll with them
My understanding is your concern
But the part that really burns
Is your empowerment
Came a little too late for me
To be able to discern
Any sense of this last decade
But yes, thank you for your honesty
I'm sure we will both thank ourselves
For it
Some day
Some how
Some way
You found your voice
And my apologies if I ever
Made it tremble and bow
Now it's bold, brazen and fearless
You are the victorious warrior
Who has gained what many
Can only dream to achieve
Even if it leaves us in a pile
Of flickering ashes

Be Kind. Please Rewind.

There is so much that has changed since 2006. That was the year my ex-wife and I started dating. Blockbuster hadn't gone out of business yet. Remember those 4 for $20 movie deals? I miss those. Beyoncé had just released her second album, *B'Day,* and Facebook was only two years old. I first met my ex-wife in 2004. We clicked right off the bat although we didn't start dating until two years later.

At that time, I was really fighting being in a relationship. I was quickly falling for her, but I tried hard not to let it show. I was fresh out of a serious relationship (and so was she). Honestly, I wasn't looking for another committed relationship. We went on a couple of dates and quickly became inseparable.

One of the best early memories I have of us is when we both worked together at the State Fair of Texas (in Dallas). I had only been in Dallas for three years at that point, so I was always excited to go to the State Fair. I started working for a promotional marketing company for part time gigs. They usually paid about $20 an hour and the work was easy. I would sell drink samples, pet supplies, household cleaners, you name it.

In the fall of 2006, I got a chance to work at the State Fair for nearly every weekend it ran. I felt like I was on top of the world. I was getting in for free, getting complimentary tickets and eating all the fried food I could get my hands on. It's funny how the simplest things meant so much back then. I told my ex-wife about it and within a couple of weeks, her and one of my close friends were working there too. They still owe her money to this day for some of the time she worked. We cracked jokes all day, ate some delicious, fattening food and got a decent check for directing people to a video simulated Nascar experience. From that point on, the State Fair was always a nostalgic time of year for us.

Although things were going well, I still tried to fight it. I didn't want to be in love again, let alone be in a new relationship. Honestly, I don't believe in changing things in the past. I'm a firm believer that everything does happen for a reason, no matter how painful it feels at the time. However, if I could go back in time, I wouldn't have taken myself so seriously. That's one major thing I would change. The older you get, there are less carefree moments. Cherish them while you can.

Hate You If I Could

Sometimes I really wish I could
Make you suffer for this failing of
A marriage that we both played our role in
This is not cool
Things went downhill far too soon
Relationships go sour, I get it
But it seems like we were
Always destined to weather the storm
But tweedle dee,
I was tweedle dumbed
To think that somehow you were
Missing me
Guess you can really know someone
Damn near half your life
And really don't know shit about em
Believe me, I would hate you if I could
But something keeps me from it
Guess it's that thing
I threw in the trash yesterday
Love

Mr. Responsibility

There is no room in the end
For Mr. Responsibility
He carries the weight
Is commended for his contributions
With a warm thank you
And a gentle hug
No matter how many facets
There are to Mr. Responsibility
He is still viewed as one dimensional
With pre-conceived notions of why
He has no need to prove himself
And if living on the edge
Helps you sleep at night
Who am I told hold you back?
Who am I to put up a fight?
Don't mistake my nonchalant demeanor
As a lack of caring
It's just me, Mr. Responsibility
Waving my white flag to surrender
Quite honestly
I'm tired of fighting

Freezing Rain

I can feel them piercing
Through the sides of my tear ducts
If only I could lock my heart
Inside of an electric cage
To stop the flow
Where no one could touch it
Especially you
And all the blood would turn
From red to purple to blue
Until it loses the oxygen
That once gave it vitality
That's exactly what I would do
Alas, these tears fall
Cold and frigid from their inception
But burning and cracking the skin
Beneath them as they roll down my face
This is a disgraceful existence
To reside in
One foot in and one foot out the door
Wondering if the wind
Will carry these tears to you
I want to turn my back to you
But I just can't make the move
I want to find myself in a new dance
But I just can't seem to pick up the groove
But you have
Maybe it's time I do the same
Instead of torturing myself with
This freezing rain

Contrary to popular belief, arguments can be healthy in a relationship.

Oh, The Rain Is Here

When it rains it pours. Right before our separation, I signed up for what I thought would be a good side job. Although I did get to pocket some of the cash, the money was fraudulent. I lost about $2000. Ouch! The next few months were a major struggle, literally and figuratively. I didn't want to have my soon to be ex-wife helping me out of this financial rut. However, she did help and offered to do even more than she did, which was nice.

My parents and best friends really stepped up and helped too. I am forever grateful for that. I felt like I was going through a huge test of my character and this was the cream cheese icing on the cake. I became very bitter and sometimes snapped at people I didn't mean to. The embarrassment and strain of being caught in a money scam was too much on top of the pending divorce.

The beginning of this book started shortly after that. At that time, I was just writing what was on my mind. Everything seemed so unfair and I kept thinking, "God, why me?" God has a way of making us eat our words and thoughts. The thoughts of "why me?" were always coupled with, "Aren't you glad it's not you?" from other people's situations going on around me.

No matter how dark it seems, if you're living and breathing, there's ALWAYS something to be thankful for. Sometimes we may never understand the reasons why certain things happen and that's ok. Life must go on.

Jealous Of Your Pillow

I am jealous of your pillow
The secrets it knows
The silent tears it holds
The way it contours to your every thought
It knows you better than I
I can only imagine that
Your pillow has a much more
Cushioned and comfortable understanding
Of those things you tried to convey to me
But I failed to comprehend
Does your pillow collect
Dreams of me now?
I often wonder
But you don't have to answer
I completely understand if you'd like to keep
That just between the two of you
Does your pillow know if we ever had real love?
Does it talk back to you and tell you when
You are being unreasonable?
Does it cradle your fears?
Does it confirm when you
Have made the right decisions?
I am jealous of your pillow
For it knows more than I ever will

Wrapped Up

I'm wrapped up in you
Whether I want to admit it or not
You were always the cold one
But lately my heart feels a little chilly too
Your threads deeply woven in my existence
Can't escape it
Every day there's a new fold
Of the tapestry that's revealed
Reminding me of what we used to be
Or what I thought it was at least
I stare at this meshed piece of fabric
Not knowing what to do with it
Do I place it in safe keeping?
Leave it on display as a reminder
Or artifact of sorts
Should I just throw it away
When I feel I can't take anymore?
Tonight, it's exceptionally cold
So, reluctantly
I wrap myself inside
And worry about the consequences
In the morning

There She Goes

There she goes
That damn newsfeed got me again
Saw your face pop up on my timeline
Felt a piece of me die inside
As I thought to myself
There goes the girl that grew into
A stunning woman that I used to know
Eyes piercing through my soul
As if you were jumping straight out
Of the picture and on my couch next to me
I resisted the urge to double tap
Say hi, what's up, you look nice
I just can't bring myself to do it
I would be communicating with
The woman I used to know
A former shell of what no longer remains
There she goes
You know her, remember?
That's what my conscious screams
But my heart pulls me back by its strings
They are tired of pulling and wearing thinner
With each rational tug of war
There she goes
But I'll just use the memories of yesterday
To soothe my mind for now

Maybe So

Maybe all I had wasn't
All I was supposed to give
Maybe I didn't give quite enough
And that's why you decided we couldn't live
And coexist under the same roof
These words hurt to write
And pain even more when they roll
Off my tongue and bounce
From the barriers of each tooth
Maybe there was more gray area
Than either you or I realized
In what was once such a black and white affair
I never thought I'd have to say maybe
On whether or not we were meant to be
Thought we'd never not know it
But seems we have been turned
Inside out and influenced by outside forces
To bring us to this place
We have so reluctantly come to be
Maybe our all wasn't enough
And it never could be
Maybe we're just exhausted
From trying to find the answers
Solve the equations
And come up with better formulas
Maybe our hearts are way past spent
To keep paying the cost of this love

Everybody is crazy. A marriage that works is about finding that one special person whose crazy is just sane enough for you to live with forever.

When Crazy Stops Making Sense

I like to think of relationships as two crazy people who like each other enough to look past each other's crazy. We are all broken, bruised and in need of healing from something. There is no such thing as a perfect mate. I always laugh to myself when I hear people say that.

People are so quick to say, "I wouldn't put up with that" or "Why do you allow her/him to treat you that way?" The truth is we all are somebody's fool. There are some things that are nonnegotiable deal breakers in a relationship for me. The next person may not believe those things are a big deal. You pick your poison in love. The hard part is when it goes sour and you must ingest it.

As I mentioned earlier, my ex-wife and I did not argue much at all. In fact, our biggest disagreements usually stemmed from what temperature we preferred. Imagine that. She liked it warm and I liked it cold. It was one of the funniest things ever (and still is). I don't think either of us can pinpoint the exact moment, but somewhere along the way our crazy stopped making sense together.

I was in denial for a long time and thought that things could still work. Unfortunately, our story played out differently. Sometimes, it's best to count your losses and move forward before things get ugly.

Backpedal

Each step I take that bridges the
Gap further between me and you
Makes me second guess if this
Is really the best thing for us to do
Just going with the flow
Playing the hand I've been dealt
Through it all I'm still trying to
Maintain my poker face
That I know you can see straight through
The sea of "what ifs" come rushing in
As they flood my mind and drown
All my rational decision-making abilities
Wait, is this really it?
Could this really be the end?
I'm not ready yet
But maybe I am
The first leap is the hardest
And this is the scariest
Leap I've ever taken in my life
Don't know if I'm going to fall flat on my face
That's why I hesitate and put it in reverse
No one wants to be the first to say goodbye
Either way, the raised skin from this scar
Will take more than a while to subside

Remember

You always did have a knack for
Selective memory
Now you are free of me
And floating in the breeze
To create new ones
With a wisp of chance
Wherever it takes you
I hope you find it
May it light your path
In times of darkness
And ignite the kind of
Excitement in your bones
That you just can't sit still
I know those memories
Will one day become faded
Though never forgotten
But I'm not sure if you will
Something tells me you'll be fine
If you don't still……remember

Let's Do It Again

I may often wonder
The reasons why, some known
Others left floating in the abyss
Of why the plug has been pulled on us
Tuesday I woke up and
Didn't want to see your face
Or even see your name on paper
By Friday I wanted to hold you close
And tell you to come over
It's a myriad of feelings on this rollercoaster
This is the big drop and I feel that queasy
Sensation brewing at the pit of my stomach
This is new, unchartered territory
That will leave some scars
That much is true
And impossible to escape
Call me a fool
Call me hopelessly in love
Or comfortability
But if I had the chance to rewind time
I'd say absolutely, unequivocally
Let's do it all again

I'd Rather Be

I'd rather be that brisk wind
That hugs your neck, unexpectedly
From behind
And makes your spine tingle
And your vision blurred
And your toes curl
Without ever being present in the room
You know, I would much rather be
The one you can't let go of
No matter how hard
You try to deny
Or pry away
From the truth
I'm in your head
And there's no escaping me
Escaping you
I don't have to be the one that
Pleasures you for a few fleeting minutes
If that is what it must be
Because orgasms go
Just as quickly as they…..come
Well, sometimes at least
I want to be the one that
Gets you all undone
And ready to revel
In that morning glory
And appreciate those things
We take for granted like breathing
Seeing beyond our eyes
Conversation that tastes so good
It makes you want to lick your lips

To savor the flavor of it for later
Or the faint rhythm of
Feeling your heartbeat through
Mere skin and a rib cage
I'd rather you never forget me
And compare every man
You ever encounter after me
And selfishly hope that they never measure up
Not in an I told you so sort of way
But in that see, you needed me kind of way
Like that big joker with the guarantee print
That you save at the end of a game of spades
And slap it on the table
Almost making everyone spill their drinks
And waiting until it's just quiet enough to speak
Ah ha, I bet you didn't see that coming, did you?
I'd rather be the one you always remember

Rip the band-aids off your love scars while they are tiny. If you don't, they become gushing wounds that can't be covered.

Stress Is A Hell Of A Drug

Some people thrive on having unnecessary drama in their lives. Thankfully, I can say I have never been in a relationship where that happened frequently. My ex-wife and I had our share of dramatic events, but neither one of us was that addicted to stress. Yes, stress is a drug too. There are some people who crave never ending break ups to make ups.

Although I wasn't a stress addict, I was guilty of being comfortable in stressful situations in my marriage. I tried to always look on the bright side of things (despite being a realist at the same time). I kept telling myself that it was just a rough patch that we would survive.

Everything started to come to a head right before we officially separated. Careers, finances and being a rock for other people can be draining enough. Throw some marital problems in the mix and it's a recipe for some spicy stress gumbo (but much less tasty).

My ex-wife started to get frequent migraines (which she never had). One day I was driving home from work and I started getting chest palpitations followed by a quick tightening that took my breath away. I thought it was strange, but just brushed it off. The feeling passed within a couple of minutes. Then it happened again a couple days later. And again. And a few more times after that. Finally, I decided I needed to get checked out by a doctor.

As I sat in the doctor's office waiting for the results of my EKG, she said, "Well, it seems like everything is fine. All your results indicate you're very healthy. Sounds like it's just stress. Monitor it for a few weeks and come back if it persists."

"Great," I thought. I just paid for a doctor's visit to only be told I'm stressed out (which I already knew). Don't get me wrong. I was grateful it was nothing major. The doctor then followed up and said, "What is it that has you so concerned?"

"Work, personal life and some other stuff," I replied nonchalantly. I think she could sense I wasn't telling the full truth.

"Something going on at home?" she asked politely. I could tell she was treading lightly, as not to pry.

"Yes, something like that. My ex-wife and I are just having a little trouble at home," I said. I flat out lied. We were past trouble. We were moving towards a divorce, but I didn't have the strength to say it then. I guess a piece of me didn't want to admit it.

I tried to relieve my stress and stay calm going forward. After all, it wasn't the end of the world (even though it felt like it at times). Then after the separation, some more things happened, and I started having these pains in the back of my head. It traveled through my shoulder and neck to the crown of my head. The best way I can describe it is like someone pulling and twisting at the muscles inside your neck and shoulders. Months later, my blood sugar count even classified me as a pre-diabetic for the first time ever. My body was telling me the harsh reality that I knew but didn't want to accept. The relationship that made so much sense had become foreign and was soon coming to an end.

Losing Ground

Losing ground never felt
So monumental
My hands are raw and scarred
From the rope burn
Losing grip on the things that
Were once so quintessential
We let love slip
Through our fingertips
Now everything is flipped
On its axis
And my new existence
Has no sturdy frame of reference
Sometimes it's best not to see you
Look in your eyes and
See the woman inside
Plus, the reflection of
The pieces of me
That have perished inside
It's just too much for
My brain to surmise
And it throws off my equilibrium
Losing that cozy, comfortable feeling
Of familiarity
Mi familia
One plus one equals three
Maybe four or five
The latter was always more your style

Oh, don't mind me
I'm just unraveling
The last of the strands of
What was lost
Pay attention so you
Don't find yourself
Losing ground like me

How Does It Taste?

I hope the flavor of your newfound freedom
Is everything you wished it would be
May it introduce your taste buds to
A new walk of life they've never known
I hope it's more decadent than you can stand
And you have to take little bites at a time
To fully appreciate it and nibble at it
In the palm of your hand
Wait, here's a glass of water
To cleanse your pallet
So you can fully explore
All those things you've previously ignored
With total leeway to delight in every day
I hope it's so mouthwatering that it
Wakes you up in the morning and
Gets you going faster
Than Folgers ever could
I hope it rocks you sound asleep
Better than a newborn baby's lullaby ever would
I hope it makes you smack your lips
And lick your fingertips
Like you forgot you were in the presence of company
At the dinner table and you were eating all alone
I hope it never finds you lonely
I hope it always puts you first
I hope it never ceases to make you smile
It better be delectable
It better be indestructible

It better be more desirable
Than the next lifetime
And you cherish it so
That you could never divide by pie
It better be so damn good
With a whipped cream cherry on top
If it means the end of you and I

On This Day

Thank you, Facebook
For reminding me of my past
My day was going just fine
Until I received the notification that said
"Remember your third anniversary dinner at Ruth's Chris"?
Great, now my heart is slammed flat on its ass
I could really use a warning
A caution or beware of sorts
Before I scroll down and see the
"On This Day" notification
For not the first, second, third
But fourth time
In one freaking day
There should be an annoying voice
Like a Gilbert Godfrey and Fran Drescher love child,
screaming
"Wait, do you really want to see this?!
It will completely ruin your day
I suggest you don't"
I could shut down my account
But that would be a bit juvenile
I could take a social media vacation
Hide out under the radar for a while
But the truth is, that won't solve a thing
Honestly, that will only delay the inevitable
I have to face the questions
The fake concerns just to get in our business
And the possibility of losing some good friends
Head on
On this day
I choose to face the truth

Smile through the pain
Laugh until it feels authentic
And live life to the fullest
Looking ahead to the kick ass
On This Day notifications I'll have
Many moons from now
At least that's the plan

Color Me Pink

Sitting here enthralled
In this beautiful trauma
Wondering how our house of cards
Fell apart
Aces first, deuces next
Just like that
Yet again, perplexed
I need a pill to numb
This strange feeling
I tell myself I'm not
Gonna let you get me
But being sober is
More frightening than
An intoxicating fantasy
We gave it a good try, didn't we?
Maybe the problem was
We spared each other's feelings
Too delicately
So what that it's over
But who am I kidding?
There is no great escape
To this madness of muddy waters
We must wade through
What do you do when
Understanding still lacks?
Stuck between you making me sick
And me saying please don't leave me
The truth about love is
It's all well and fine
Until that unexpected blow
Knocks you right between the eyes

Boy Toy

I hope you're able to find
One right off the shelf
That does all the things I did and more
I hope he comes with no defects
Or factory malfunctions
He can be your life sized
Soldier, ready and at attention
To be all the man you mold him out to be
I hope you'll be able to wind him up
To make you laugh with the deepest joy
Like an earthquake that rattles your soul
Without the messy aftershock
I hope he comes with a manufacturer's warranty
Just in case one of his parts breaks off
Or he doesn't obey your voice commands
Or fails to move with the swiftness you need him to
I hope you save your receipt
Just in case you might need it
As your proof of purchase
And get a refund
But in the event that
He must be placed back
On the shelf
In rewrapped shiny new packaging
And refurbished parts
I'll be long gone
Because I simply don't
Have the heart

Chandelier

Look up to the ceiling
And see the breathtaking mess we made
Dripping with intricate details
Gleaming the sun's brightest rays
At first glance it looks breathtaking
Like a sugar rush mixed with a nice buzz
But take a closer look to see
The diamonds, gems and precious metals
Were bonded with blood and tears
It's a gorgeous, frightening masterpiece
Hoovering above our heads
Like a rain cloud mixed with sunshine
That we just can't escape
I saw it coming this time
So I packed my umbrella today
In case the glorious reign is
Too much to bear
Even in the dark
It deflects light from any angle
They will have to study it for hours
To find out how we made it
And even then they still
won't figure it out
This house is empty
The only emblem of love
Is the evidence of our
Hearts, minds and souls shifting
With this custom, one of a kind chandelier
Dangling from the ceiling
I wonder what they will make of it

Relationships are not just between two people, rather they are the sum of the lasting impacts of everyone who has inspired or hurt them.

Stay Woke

Relationships take work. I think it's safe to say we have all heard that before. Although it's extremely cliché, it's true. There's a saying ("stay woke") that many people in the African American community have used in recent years, related to paying attention to social injustice. One of the greatest lessons I learned from my marriage is that you must stay woke.

Before my ex-wife, I never had a girlfriend for longer than a year. Granted, I was only 21 when we first started dating. Neither one of us really got to live life because we were both busy being so responsible. Then, our relationship became a focus. Careers, school, my writing, her acting and eventually building a life together consumed all our twenties. Everything happened in the blink of an eye. Before I knew it, the crux of my youth had floated by.

Through it all, you have to continue to pay attention. I'm not the same guy I was at 30 years old, 25 and certainly not 21. My ex-wife was evolving too. We were two people who were growing and changing; not always in the same direction either. Often, it's easy to get comfortable in a marriage. By that point, you pretty much know the person's habits, their likes and dislikes.

However, there is danger in that comfortability. People change and what you think you know soon becomes new aspects of the same person. Take it from me. One of the keys to keeping a marriage running like a well-oiled machine is knowing what makes the other person tick, even if that means throwing away everything you thought you previously knew. Isn't it ironic how we learn so much when we look back, but lose focus while we're in it? Pay attention and when you think you've learned all there is to know, pay attention again. Stay woke.

Worth A Thousand Words

Today, I took your bridal portrait
Off my desk at work
At this point, the possibility of divorce
Had been introduced over 100 days ago
The imprint had been set in something
Between play doh and cement for over 40 days
Prior to today, I lied and participated in
Conversations about how it feels to be married
Knowing that pretty soon
I would not have a seat at that table
I cringed when couples talked about their
Cute little babies or planning for their next one
A piece of me burns inside
That this is not the story for you and I
I am not embarrassed
Divorces happen every day right?
I just don't want the questions
The poking and prodding
And why and how
But I think they already know
I haven't worn my ring in two weeks
Maybe I'm a bit narcissistic to even believe
They are paying attention or even care
I took your picture out of my work bag
Laid it on the front seat, face up
Glancing at it the whole way home
At times, restricted myself not to smash it

With the hammer in my back seat
As I reluctantly faced the chilling pain
That our existence has been diminished
To moments like this
High resolution prints of memories
We once shared together

And The Awards Goes To

Let me stand to my feet
Turn on all the lights
So I can see the beams bounce
And gleam from your teeth
As you pour out your acceptance speech
This has got to be the longest
Anyone has ever stayed in character
Known to man
No, its ok I don't need to
Stand with you on this one
Or be there to hold your hand
You have earned your trophy
And all its radiant splendor
The cooler I played it
The more tenacious your role became
And you executed your part with vigor
I figure if it makes you happy
Then you enjoy the mirage
I could sprawl the collage
Of memories across the floor
As your red carpet for you to walk on
Is that what you would like?
After all, you are the queen of the night
Oh, what a time to wear a guise
What a time to be alive

Limbo

How low can we go?
I think I would rather not know
If this is rock bottom
Shoot me up to where the stars go
Propel me high above the sickening
Facades and niceties
Of trying to salvage the remnants
Of our love that is stuck to the bottom
Of the barrel
How low can we go?
I would rather not stoop down
To the floor to try to pick up
The shards of our complicated brokenness
I don't want to get cut
I don't want to be let down
I don't want to contort myself under
Weak possibilities
Only to fall flat on the ground
How low can we go?
Let's stop here because
I'd rather that neither one of us
Ever has to know

Delusions Of The Third

Let's do the math
Like one plus one equals three
And the name of our first born
That we never will get to meet
You wanted three
I was always happy
With two or just one
Hey, I came out alright, right?
Now I don't know after
346, 896,000 seconds
4015 days
132 months
Poof, just like that
It's all up in smoke
A burning stench in the air
No store credit for all these years
Or even a stinking IOU
33 percent of my life
Is a long time to eventually waste
Though I know there's a reason
It's just not how it feels
Or what I want to hear
When all the things
You thought you knew
Become undone
I am a delusional mess

Be careful of the words you speak over your relationship and your significant other. Those words frequently become thoughts, eventually manifesting themselves into actions.

Turning In The Keys

I don't proclaim to be an avid student of numerology. However, I believe there is great power in numbers. Numbers have often been used to confirm many important things in my life. Before I was married, I lived in three apartments back to back where the apartment number equaled nine. All three of those apartments really felt like home.

For a few years afterwards, I put less value in the address of my residence equaling nine. Maybe it wasn't all it was cracked up to be in my head. Seven is another very important number in my life. The number seven seems to follow me, as far back as my birthday (I was born exactly seven days after my due date). I was the seventh person to enter my undergraduate chapter of Alpha Phi Alpha Fraternity, Inc. It seemed there was no escaping the presence of seven in my life.

Fast forward to the final day of the lease for the apartment that my ex-wife and I shared. I had already moved out a few weeks prior. Whenever we would see each other, I felt a wave of emotions. I believe she may have felt the same. The end of a relationship is much like the grieving process of a death. You go through all the stages of denial, anger, bargaining, depression and acceptance.

If I am being completely honest with myself, the stage I felt the strongest and most often was depression. The others came and went sporadically at various times. I felt all five feelings at once that day. I didn't know what to say or how to act. The feeling was like being the new kid on that first day of school, but much worse. I would like to think that we both handled the situation well. We even cracked a couple of jokes at some points; just like old times. No matter how bad a situation is, I try to find some humor in it. As I reflected on the whole interaction on the way home, it hit me. The address for our apartment equaled the number seven. It was a sign of completion. I never even paid attention to it until then. That day, I turned in the keys to an apartment we shared, but also to the life I had become so familiar with for the past eleven years.

Heartburn

Is it your idea of fun
To stimulate this
Fiery sensation in my chest?
Do you get a kick out of watching
My soul squirm as I learn
How to adjust to this table of one?
Does your pulse begin to rise
When you look at me
And see all the things we were
Evaporate like the sun
Drying up all the rain
From the tears on these pages?
Lately, I've rarely shown them
Would it be uncouth of me to
Pretend I am aloof to remembering
All the minute details
I would rather not hold on to
The acid is rising
It's getting harder to breathe
Boiling with no outlet
For love's steam
I dream that one day
All the stars will align
And this heartburn
Will finally subside

Choked Up

There's something about
The way you look at me
With those doe, pretty brown eyes
You know I see you and
They stop me dead in my tracks
My head gets light and
My throat gets tight
And it gets hard to breathe
Imagining you not being here at night
But what kind of man would I be
By keeping you prisoner in a cage
That you demand to be set free from
Fly high
Spread your wings
I'll be alright
I think
I hope
I believe
I have no other choice but to be
As the time draws nigh
I can't look in those doe baby
Pretty brown eyes
Cause in them I see
Nothing but our demise
Gets me so choked up
So, I just look the other way

Here's Looking At You

Today I saw an older man
While I was people watching
As I often do
Still seemed full of vitality
I guessed he was probably 62
He seemed content as he read
And waited for no one in particular
I fought the urge to ask why he was there
Was it just a leisure point along the way
To his next destination?
Was he headed to bible study?
Nope, it was a Monday
So that was highly unlikely
I wondered did he have a family
Wife and maybe kids
With kids of their own
Or was he through with love
And just content in his own company?
I was afraid to ask
Not because I was too shy to pry
Into the life of a stranger
But because I didn't want him to potentially
Confirm the person I'd see in the mirror
Years from now

Distraction

Distractions aren't healthy
But I'm not looking for mixed greens
Or anything of the sort, right now
I need something to
Soothe my heart somehow
Even if it clogs my arteries
Because my muscles are already
Stretched way past their capacity as it is
I know it will only be a band aid
I know that once the morning returns
I'll be back at square one
I know that this isn't the mature way
To handle to it
This isn't the best way I'll get over it
But I just want a sip
Hell, even a hit to push
This broken love out my mind
The way I'm set up it will become
Just another bad habit to overcome
Though the struggle of being an addict
Would be a spectacular one
Compared to this dark, twisted nightmare
I'm suspended in now
Only hope it doesn't cut me too badly
On the way out
But my soul is already slashed
So what's another gash?
I can take the pain
I have endured this
They'll say I'm weak for not standing up
To my issues, face to face

But I don't give a damn what they say
Cause they don't have to bear
The still, thick silence in the night
I need something to make my toes curl
I need something to inspire me
I need something to ignite and excite me
Make me laugh til I cry
Just until this dark cloud subsides
Anybody know where I can
Find a distraction of this fashion?

If you fail to fully love yourself, you will never be able to completely love someone else.

The Definition

I believe that you should not let a relationship define who you are. However, a marriage treads that fine line. A marriage is more than just a relationship that you can leave when you want to. It is the pinnacle of commitment, for life. So, it does in a sense define who you are; at least to the public.

Although my ex-wife and I were married for less than five years, we were together for eleven. When people hear about a failed marriage that's less than five years old, they barely cringe. After all, divorce rates are at an all time high. However, when you add in the total sum of a relationship, the jaws start dropping. The story suddenly takes a different turn.

I once had someone ask me if I was going to delete all the pictures on social media of my ex-wife and I together. I thought the question was so ludicrous that I literally laughed out loud. How do you erase eleven years of memories? You can't. Sure, you can delete photos, but that's childish. My ex-wife was a huge part of my life. I spent nearly one third of my entire life with her. My answer was simply, "No".

The definition of who I was becoming was changing. Nonetheless, I was unable to detach my ex-wife from who I had been for the last eleven years. Did my marriage define me as a person? No, but it surely was a huge part of who I was. I am not ashamed of that definition changing.

Where Is My Receipt?

I get that I'm not who you thought I was
We weren't who you thought you were
And you weren't willing to sacrifice
What you thought would hurt
I really don't get it
But we'll just say that I do
I just have one question for you
What do I do with all these memories?
Do I just save them as historical currency
Like washed up encyclopedias
Readily available for information
That is useless to us now?
Maybe I'm supposed to sweep them under the rug
Along with the frayed particles of my dignity
I refuse to lose my cool though
Because it won't bring us back to the place
That never was
I am smiling, but I am seething inside at times
I am smiling, but I am hopeful inside that I
Will learn some valuable golden nugget
From this crock of fool's gold
I am smiling, but nothing is happy right now
I stretch the skin on my forehead
As not to relay the furrowed brow
My brain wants to convey
To my facial muscles to make
I lied
I have one more question
Can you give me a receipt
For all this time we wasted?

Syrup

It's dripping down my chin
My tongue peruses my upper lip
As I savor the flavor
And the slow roll down my neck
I don't bother to wipe it off
Let it stay right there
Elated to have you right there
It's a nectar sweeter than anything
My taste buds have ever experienced
I don't mind getting a little messy in it
Because the best things in life
Hardly ever come clean
I was down in the trenches with you
I was down for the fight
Yeah it's true
Even when the syrup turned toxic
Splattered on my heart
Bruised and bludgeoned with boils
But I was cool
Because love doesn't come easy
Or at least that's what they tell me
I was willing to trudge through it
Until this syrup transformed
Into a scorching, sticky situation
Damn I remember the inviolate substance
Before we compromised it
With all the fillers and preservatives
My soul feels deserted
But I'm getting used to the company

Slumped in this corner
Watching the last drop of
The syrup seep out of love's edifice

All The Things You Hate

Today I inhaled and took a whiff
Of the cologne you never liked
Made me crack a smile
So I put on another spritz
Hoped you would smell it across town
And remember all the things you miss
I stepped out of the shower and
Left the floor all wet
Like you would come in behind me
And tell me to dry my feet off
Before I take another step
I slept with the covers off
And turned the AC down past a cool breeze
Hoping it would wake you out of your sleep
And feel how my heart has turned cold
I blasted the speakers to my stereo
As soon as I turned the key
And walked inside my new home
You never liked all that noise
And preferred the subtle murmur
Of your favorite TV shows
I turned up the bass another notch
Enough to rattle your brain
With hope that somewhere in there
You could retain
Some sense of respect for me and us
I stayed out all night
Until the street lights dimmed
And tip toed in silently
Like I had someone to answer to
So you could see how it feels

But oops, I forgot we no longer share
The same personal space
Since I can't be all the things you love
I'll settle for being all the things you hate

Hearts Bleed

Hearts bleed, at times profusely
If you're lucky, you save yourself before
You lose too much of the essence of your being
Hearts bleed, at times steadily
And if you're ever so lucky
A true friend will be there to help you clean
The mess from crimson stains
And restore your soul to its original hue
Someone come quickly
Because this heart is bleeding
Hearts bleed and hearts get bruised
When they are taken out of their natural element
Which can turn them black and blue
Sometimes hearts bleed and it's just a nick
A needle-sharp prick
That doesn't need much mending
Or tedious tending to
Some hearts stay away from
Familiar trauma
Because the thought of repeating
The chalky, bitter flavor
Of rehabilitation is more than an ocean
To swallow
Some hearts wallow in their
Self-inflicted wounds
Wondering how it all became undone
Hearts bleed at the most inopportune moments
Like spilling red wine on your shirt
At an all-white party
Where's the glory in that?
If you're lucky, you get to cleanse it in time

To possibly wear that shirt again
Someday
Hearts bleed
It's a part of life
Hearts bleed
And sometimes we can't see
The blood dripping on top of our shoe
From the person standing
Right next to us
Because truthfully we're all scrambling
For gauze to treat our own wounds
Hearts bleed
If you're lucky
You get knocked down, get picked up
Stop the bleeding
Restore all the necessary functions
And share life with those
Who once had or still do
Have hearts that bleed too

There's a fine line between possessiveness and jealousy. Tow it with caution.

What Really Happened?

As more people started to find out about my divorce, I began to get good at predicting their questions. Pretty soon, the conversations were cookie cutter and I learned to phrase my answers accordingly. Whenever a relationship ends, specifically a marriage, people always feel the need to get to the root cause of the blame. He must have been at fault. She must have been a fault.

A relationship takes two. I like to believe that most people do not get involved in a relationship (let alone a marriage) with the thought of it eventually ending. Even the most abusive relationship has two sides. True, the person who is supplying the abuse is in the wrong, without a doubt. However, the person accepting it plays a role too because they allow it. Of course, this is a rather harsh example; but it's true.

I never bad mouthed my ex-wife to my family, friends or associates. I believe she did the same regarding me. The truth is the marriage came to a crossroads beyond our repair. There was no bad guy (or woman). Were there things I did wrong? Heck yeah. Were there things she did wrong? Yes.

Nonetheless, when people love you, they care for your well-being. They want to get to the source of your pain. The truth is, my ex-wife is nothing short of an amazing woman. We just uncovered some non-negotiables in our marriage that ultimately led to it imploding. That's my story and I'm sticking to it.

Freckles

I hold her face in my dreams
Lately I've had a feeling that it
Would have been a gorgeous little girl
We already had her name picked out
At least you won't get to create her
With anyone else, no doubt
But I will let that go
Because what has happened
Transpired for a reason, I know
It was out of my control
But her little smile
Warms my heart and the room
She's a delicate flower in full blown
I know she would have been something special
Spunky like her mother
And probably have my stubborn ways
I can see her dancing for days, like you
Instead, I can only imagine her gaze
Her breath so near, I can feel it
Against my chest
She would have been so intelligent
With a face to melt the masses
And freckles, just like her mother

Walking Egg Shell

A walking egg shell cannot walk in the rain
That rain may turn to hail and
Pierce it's exoskeleton
So, it often walks with an umbrella
Even when the sun is shining
A walking egg shell must steer clear
Of windows during tornadoes
Because the building could rock
The glass could shatter
And blow the egg shell to shards and pieces
A walking egg shell never quite learns to
Breathe easy, gathering the fresh oxygen
Beneath oak trees
There may be birds up there waiting
To swoop down and
Poke, prod and peck with their beaks
I am that walking egg shell
Dodging inquiries and familiar faces
As though not to break
I am that walking egg shell that needs
A seat to rest my mind
But there is no mold safe enough to fold into
Yesterday, I was that walking egg shell
But today I am walking boldly
Exposed, unprotected,
Maybe my strength was undetected
And I wasn't the walking egg shell
I thought I was cracked up to be

Now. Then. See You Later

We used to taste so divine
At least to me
Until sour turned to bitter
And there was nothing sweet
Between you and me
All the ingredients left
Strewn across the floor
I pick them up one by one
Dust them off
Melt them all together
In the pot
Then simmer them slow
Give them the best that I got
But my best wasn't enough to bring
Back what would soon become
The unsavory flavors of these now and laters
If I was a little more tender back then
Maybe things would be sweeter now
If I understood the impact of what would
Happen later
Maybe I could have done something
During the now back then
But we can't pretend
Or hope to mend the words and actions
We have consumed
From one another
And that's just it
Maybe my best was mediocre at most
This love is comatose
These flavors are downright gross
Like too much cumin on

Chicken wings and potatoes
Now, we are that mystery flavor
You pray to always miss
When you scoop a handful
With your fingertips
In the bag, there are no more tricks
There are no more kisses and hugs
Just relentless shrugs
And two monumental ideals
That will not budge or
Merge for the common good
I never thought our
Now, back then
Would end up tasting so dreadful later

Try Love At Your Own Risk

Try love, they say
It will be the most exhilarating thing
In the world
Better than diamonds and pearls
Love has its ups and downs, they say
But that love you have
For each other
Will be enough to calm
The motion in the ocean
Bring it to a still, small sway
Easy like Sunday morning
In a rocking chair
Yet Sundays became rocky
Turbulent and uneasy
What happened to the
Sweet, savory and satiating taste of love
They said we'd devour
From delicious to degradation
There is no careful trepidation
They didn't tell us about
The scorch that burned our hunger
And bitterness that soured our hearts
Hold hands, they say
Kiss under the mistletoe, they say
Make love in open fields, under the stars
They say
These are the makings of love
Too bad they didn't tell us
That sustaining love
Requires more than the
Birds and bees

Honey-do lists and
Always remembering to say please
It's work and pain and tears
Fighting through your biggest fears
And joy and smiles with ignorant bliss
Love can be the biggest pile of…..
If you let it
So, if you can't fit love
On your plate and dive into the
Full course meal exactly as it was prepared
With no conditions, alterations or exclusions
Don't even bother to
Have a seat at the table

Marriage is a compromise: sometimes you have to be okay with getting the short end of said compromise.

Going Through Withdrawals

I personally don't believe that you can ever rid yourself "clean" of a long-term relationship, especially a marriage. This doesn't mean that you wallow in the way things were (or however you thought they were). However, it's still a memory; even if it eventually becomes a distant one. All of this is new to me, so I can't really say how I will feel a year from now, five years from now or ten years from now.

The truth is if you really had love for the person that you were married to, the love is still there. My ex-wife and I were blessed, all things considered, to not go through some things other couples did. Many divorced people that I know say that they do still have love for their ex-spouse. I get a kick out of some people who act like they hate their ex-husband or wife. Hate came from love at some point and it's often a sign that the person hasn't moved on.

There have been times I laughed to myself thinking about some of my ex-wife's favorite songs, foods or movies. Those memories sucker punch me in the gut at the most unexpected times. Sometimes it really stings and others it brings a smile to my face. Although we are not together anymore, there is a piece of both of us that is still right there, just like we never left.

How Are You?

The cat has clawed
Scratched and yelled way past
A mere meow
And now it's all out the bag
It's all over the floor
I could damn near predict
What happens next, verbatim
They look
Their eyes lock with mine
Move left to right
Their mouth opens
Wide at first
Until they catch themselves
Then they close it
Their lips part
Just wide enough to
Take a sip of water
To quench their nosy ass thirst
"Well, what happened?"
"Ok, I get it. That's so unfortunate"
"Have you sought counseling?"
"Maybe things will turn around?"
"Exactly when did your world together
Turn upside down?"
"I just can't take this"
Now I'm handing them a tissue
For my own problems
Well isn't this just the
Freaking dream?
For people to know
All your business

Or at least what they see
On the surface
From fragmented pieces of the puzzle
And now they are putting it all back together
Trying to tell you what it all means
How am I?
I'm well past fed up with people
Inviting me to their couch
For therapy that I never asked to sit on
Thank you for your concern
But I'd rather you not even care
If your intentions are untrue

Skin To Skin

I lay staring at the ceiling
Wondering if you're still awake
In the same bed
Skin to skin
But it feels like there's a stranger
Lying next to me
No longer those carefree kids
Innocence stripped as we've
Been through too much
On our own and together
Slow to trust
I don't think either one of us
Wanted our story to combust
Like this, shards of sharp memories
Suspended in the air
That resemble confetti
Right before they cut like a knife
When they fall from the sky
The thunder rolls and I wonder
If there was any way we
Could have pushed this storm
Due south and dodged it
To get back to the people we knew
The particles of our love
Slipped through our fingers
Like sand through an hourglass
It's an hour past the credits and
I'm still holding on
Like at the end
Of those Marvel movies for some kind of
Clue or a sequel to the next chapter of my life

Ayanla can't fix it
Neither can you
Neither can I
The show is over
We must take the bow
And turn down the lights

Labor Of Love

The 27th of apprehension
About the contention
Of this decision
No takebacks now
No more wash backs
From your juice to
My lips
How did we get here?
Seems we already know
Yet, we don't really know….
If we did, maybe our ending
Wouldn't have played out quite like this
You didn't believe in death
Said we would just teleport
Up to heaven like beams
In the sky, simultaneously
Yet, here we are
The glue that once held our hearts
Is now a wedded mirage
With the dirt, indefinitely
I'd like to think we gave it
One hell of an earnest fight
But sometimes the most
Intense labor of love
Still isn't enough
To make everything alright

Forgiving Us

I'll be honest. I've been guilty of holding a grudge or two in the past. I over analyze many situations in life, which is not always the best thing to do. However, when I finalize a decision, I usually move forward in that direction without wavering. By that time, I have looked at more possibilities than a Rubik's cube. It's important to know yourself and I'm fully aware of the intricacies of my inner thoughts. I'm working on forgiving quicker and becoming unoffendable. As we all are, I'm still a work in progress.

The stages of getting over a breakup (especially a divorce) are not necessarily sequential. The acceptance may come early, even before anger does. Bargaining may come after acceptance. At some points, I didn't know how I was going to feel from one moment to the next.

Sundays were always an awkward time towards the end of my ex-wife and I's marriage. One Sunday, after we separated, I went to church and heard a sermon about being unoffendable. Have you ever found yourself at the right place at the right time, but didn't realize it until after you left? Well, that was me on that Sunday. I realized there were still some things I hadn't forgiven my ex-wife for.

Don't get me wrong. I know I can be a handful. While we were engaged, my ex-wife and I took the love languages test from the book, *The 5 Love Languages*. My ex-wife scored high on the areas of physical touch and quality time. Guess what my love language was? All five! I virtually had a five-way tie. We often laughed about it long after we took the test.

As unoffendable as we try to be, sometimes the person we offend the most is ourselves. I realized that to heal from my broken marriage, I had to forgive myself first before my ex-wife or anyone else. When a marriage ends, there is always something both parties could have done better. That's just life. My newfound realization was bittersweet. I purged through my thoughts yet again; but the fact that there was still a purge to get through opened some old scabs all over again.

Same Ole Love

I once wanted that same ole love
Those same ole hugs and kisses
Like we used to
You know when it was just us two
Until I learned that same ole love
Wasn't what it was
A fossil of representation
Of a dried-up love
That wiggled astray
Before it was even our own to stay
Yet, here I am dreaming
Of that same ole love
Here I am naively thinking
It was that weather the storm love
That whenever things got turbulent
We held on for dear life love
That peanut butter jelly
We belong together, love
Damn, I am exhausted, love
Now that same ole love
I once wished for
Is foreign, fragile and damaged
Beyond belief
I pray to keep
And grit my teeth
If you ever believed
I wasn't listening intently enough
I apologize to you, me and us
There goes that same ole love
Tip toeing right out the back door
You were right

Whether by sheer ignorance
Or my own selective memory
I never heard your cry to mend love
Until those words trampled on my heart
And broke it, love
I will now refrain from wishing
For a same ole love
That apparently never was
Love is closed for business
Until further notice
I ignored my first mind, love
Put my fears aside, love
Took the punches in stride, love
Paid the consequence for mistakes, love
Nobody's perfect, love
You look in my eyes
Only seeing a still disguise
Windows through a house
That is not a home
There's no light here
To be turned on
There's a vacancy
Love has left the building
All its complicated imperfections
Have left right along with it

Insomniac

I lie awake
Mind racing and pacing
Like all the brainiacs
With no pinkys
Who flip through almanacs
I'm quite detached from reality
As the tune brings me back
To summers that ignited the
The most passionate itchy scratch
Codes for inside jokes
That you just can't crack
And then splat
When it all falls down
Damn, for real?
Yeah, just like that
Immersed in fictitious facts
I am purple blue black
Click clack go the chambers
Stacked and hollow
Keys disposed
I still lie awake
Mind still racing, pacing
Like all those brainiacs
Who lost their pinkys
And have nothing better to do
Than flip through their stacks of almanacs
I too am quite detached from reality
I supposed
Day 21 add a zero
No savage

This has got to be lavish insanity
Where's pinky when you need him?
I'm still awake

Be careful who and what you vent to when your relationship is going through a rough patch. It's better to keep your lips sealed and your fingers still.

Speak No Evil

Throughout the separation and the divorce process, I primarily kept to myself. I used the time to sort out my thoughts, improve personally and really try to figure out what my next step in life was going to be. I'm still figuring that part out now, which isn't an easy task when you've shared your life with someone else for over a decade. However, one of the best things I did was keep my mouth shut.

Many people don't realize that emotionally vomiting about a breakup (let alone a divorce) to followers on social media, family and friends only backfires in the long run. I've seen it happen to more people than I can count. Some people get back together and look silly because they have talked about each other like dogs. Then, there are times people say things that were only mentioned in a heated moment to an associate or friend. The word travels back to the other party and before you know it, the broken couple hates each other over a stretched truth (people always add more to a story when they tell it).

On my worst days, I became somewhat of a hermit. I would go to work and then just come home. You may read this and think it sounds depressing. However, I looked at it as staying out of the line of fire. People love to hear negativity and I was determined not to be the subject of anyone's happy hour gossip (at least not by my own doing). I didn't have much control over my life at the time, but I could at least control my mouth.

I have found that strangers are often the best people to talk to about situations like this. Family and friends are needed, but those waters can get muddy quickly. Family usually sides with their own, which may not end well if they ever run into the other person again. Friends are tricky too, especially if you shared mutual friendship. Those people may end up feeling caught in the middle and forced to pick a side. Strangers have no vested interest in our lives though. Often, a stranger can help you see the situation from a big picture view, without any bias.

The moral of the story is be careful who you tell your business to. It's much easier to keep silent rather than desperately trying to retract words that have already been said.

Cherry Cordial

We've kept it eerily copacetic
Like the final five seconds
Counting down before
The bomb detonates
Don't mistake my restraint
As being synonymous
With my love imploding for you
And not exploding
It's still there, standing tall
But wise enough to set you free
We've kept it so cherry cordial
I always did like that flavor
But things taste so different
Bittersweet and sour now
The whipped cream on top
Can't even save us
How do we remain so cool?

It's A Different World Now

"Blessed are those who ask the questions brother!" This is a quote from one of my ex-wife's favorite TV shows, *A Different World*. The episode details one of the main characters, Dwayne, speaking up against his true love, Whitley, getting married. To ask that question is a loaded one to say the least. Requesting another person to share your life (for the rest of your life) is no small feat.

I wondered what was supposed to be my reason for asking the question. It obviously wasn't for forever. However, I couldn't be settled with the possibility that I was supposed to learn some grand lesson from an eleven-year relationship. Couldn't I have learned the lesson in year three or four? Before the attachment grew stronger? Before the wedding and the shared debt? I guess God has a sense of humor.

Honestly, I probably wouldn't change anything to make this moment come sooner. Everything was meant to happen the way it was designed to. I still consider my ex-wife a great friend and there's no way I could erase all the memories we shared, even if I tried. Oh and during my angry days, I tried. But it didn't work. I finally realized it never could. Through the amazing highs and profound lows, our time together was meant to be.

Yellow Grass

I can only imagine
How plush and invigorating the
Dirt beneath those vibrant green
Blades of grass must feel
Between your toes
Just barely tickling the bottom
Of your ankles
As the sun subtly bakes your skin
And fills your heart with a warm glow
Like you've never known
But, if you find those blades
Start to change their hue
Transform their texture
And fully depleted of their moisture
Just look up and there you will see
I will be waiving from the other side
Where the grass is greener

Relationship Goals

I think I would be perfectly fine
If I never heard the phrase
Relationship goals in my life again
I know what you're thinking
I'm bitter and sinking into
Self-inflicted solitude
From my failed marriage
And I am just trying to find a
Willing roommate to keep me company
But that's where you're wrong
Because pictures only expose
Filters, tropical backgrounds, perfect angles
Body enhancements, shades to cover black eyes
Or dark circles from the lack of sleep at night
Like your side of the bed that's cold
From staying out too late
Or the echoes bouncing off the walls
From stale arguments
And weighing out all your options to
See if it's worth it to stay
They present only what the couple
Achieving these goals allows you to see
But not what lies beneath
Don't believe the hype
The most sought-after goals from
A successful relationship
Were not cultivated over night

So, let's stop the lies
And refrain from always
Striving to be like Mike….and what's her name
As for me and my house
I'm only focused on being the best, me myself and I
And if, by chance, I ever fall in love again
She will be just the same

Bring Back The Shadows

It's pitch black, feet flat
Walking on rock bottom's back
Damp with discernment
Forgiveness is somewhere
Suspended in the balance
But I can't see it
Seems like every move I take
I'm running into another wall
Every ascending step
Begets another tumultuous fall
I can hear my breath echoing
Inside this tiny cage that
Used to enclose a malleable heart
Now I'm just throwing darts
In the dark
You are here somewhere too
In this labyrinth of love's destruction
But I can't get to you
Barbed wire fences separate us
And requiring you and me
To sacrifice more of ourselves than
We are willing to possibly arrive at
The epicenter of some semblance of normalcy
No I can't see anything surrounding me
Somebody bring back the shadows
With just enough light to guide me
Where I'm supposed to be

Water With No Lemons

One thing that really gets on my nerves is to see actively bitter people talking down on someone else's marriage or relationship. Believe me, I had some bitter days during my divorce. However, I was determined not to be that person. Instead, I openly congratulated people who were engaged and even randomly asked some associates how their spouses were doing.

You may be reading this thinking, "That's over the top". I don't see it that way though. Love is a wonderful thing and people who have been scarred by it have no right to taint it for others. Misery loves company. Sometimes, it's easy to fall into the trap of picking apart someone else's relationship when yours has gone to shambles. I like to take the "If you ask, I'll tell approach". During the period of my divorce, I was tight lipped about other people's relationships around me. If they asked, I gave them my honest opinion (which at times was unfavorable). Nonetheless, I avoided readily offering my two cents.

Love is supposed to be pure and not polluted with bitter perspectives. We all have different experiences. Plus, I never want to receive the karma of judging other people's relationships. If they like it, I love it. Honestly, I have more important things to focus on than negatively inserting myself into someone else's love life.

Grim Reaper

Sometimes I wish
I could retrace my steps
The ones leading up to
Walking down that aisle
I wonder if He saw it
Coming to an end
Before it even began
Like we didn't
I wonder what He thinks about us
Breaking our promise so easily
Truthfully
I fought all I could
Honestly
I gave all that I would
Because some things just
Leave you permanently shook
Like color combinations of yellow and grey
Or the big smile on your face
As the saxophone played
To your entrance on our wedding day
We did not fulfill the covenant
Things got so misty
I could barely tell if
He was still in the room sometimes
He knows my heart
And that's what keeps me restless
I am the grim reaper in the flesh
Just living and vibrant
Awaiting to see what we will reap from this
Standing tall, yet timidly
With relief and regret

I put my hands over my face
Peeking through the cracks
Cause I don't want to see
His disapproving look
His gaze piercing through my soul
I know I can't hide
He gave us free will to decide
The grimace of broken rings
Is what I see when I look
Outside my window
Now I must wait patiently to see
What I reap from
The venom of this decisive sting

October 31st

I doubt that even just a penny
For your thoughts
Would make me anymore the wiser
I never considered myself
To be a Georgie Porgie
Yet the tears keep rolling down your cheeks
I can still hear the screech of those words
Scratched against my eardrums
Like Edward Scissorhands
Running his nails across
A three-dimensional chalkboard
Afraid to look at myself in the mirror
Hearing your name resonate in the dark
Like Candyman, say it three times
And run for your life
So I keep this smile on
Unshakeable, unbreakable
The heartiness of my laugh
May rival Dr. Giggles
But I know I'm out of my mind
Just in time
All while keeping a poker face
I do not come dressed in costume
I embody it
Become one with it
My second skin
Transposes with my first
Like Michael Myers
Just without the erratic outbursts
Chasing myself slowly like Jason
Placing this mask on, year round

Lights On, Lights Off

You were that kind of peace
In a groove
On a Sunday afternoon
That took my breath away
Oh yes, you did
Soon, yet far away
We would become pieces
Broken, trying desperately to find
That sweet groove again
I left the light on
When things got too deep
And you couldn't see
I left it on at night
Like a bat signal in the sky
A lighthouse of sorts
To guide your way and let you know
I was still in this for the long haul
I left it on in the morning
When I knew the night before
Might have kicked your ass a little too hard
To raise your head
And coherently pull yourself out of bed
Yes, it might have kicked your ass a little too hard
For that is something I will
Likely never know
I left that light on perpetually
I left that light on when I knew
My better judgment was telling me not to
I left that light on day in and into the night
I left that light on
Before the sun awakened

And danced upon your eyelids
No matter how hard you tried
To block it out
I left that light on for you
Tonight, I'm turning it off for me

Love doesn't change the characteristics that reside in a person's core.

No Price Tag For Peace

I remember one of the first days I started to sink into acceptance that my marriage was really coming to an end. I say "one of the first" because the process really has been a rollercoaster of emotions. Some days are full of denial, anger, bargaining or even depression. On that day, I had $11.56 in my bank account. Oh, let me not forget the $5 in cash too.

Although I was still recovering from the fraudulent activity that depleted my bank account, I was happy. No, I was at peace. Happiness is fleeting, but peace cannot be shaken by life's situations. You may be wondering how in the world I found peace with so little money and a pending divorce. Good question. When I find out the answer, I'll be sure to let you know. All I can say is God allowed it to happen.

I honestly didn't care where my newfound peace came from. I was just glad that it arrived. Sure, I had some happy and joyous moments, but this was the first time I experienced true peace in a long time. The stress about my financial situation and my divorce could have kept me in an acrimonious state of mind. I had plenty of those days too. In fact, I still have them now.

However, the amazing thing about finally finding peace is even if you lose it (or think you have) for a time, you can find your way back to it. That day, I had an inkling of what really gave me my peace. More importantly, I figured out that I had the power to hold on to it.

I Don't Know

People often ask me
How you've been
I quickly change my expression
And my first inclination to say
"Your guess is as good as mine"
Or "How the hell should I know"?
I just saw you last week
But I realize that the look in your eyes
Is one I don't quite recognize
And all those things
I thought I knew have subsided
Far beneath the shore
Far away from view
Isn't it true
When you look at me
And see the same?
Oh what a great disdain
A rolling, numbing pain
To realize that the one
That you used to be able to
Know through and through
Completed their sentences
Knew their favorite songs
And all their favorite foods
Has changed
When they ask what I know
I smile and reply with
An answer that comfortably fits
The likeness of who I remember you to be
But let's not fool ourselves, shall we

You are no longer her
And he is no longer me
Who knows if what I know
Can be unpacked with the same validity
As it once did

Happy Birthday

Sitting here contemplating
Seething a little bit
Well, who am I fooling
Angry a lotta bit
It's your birthday and I'm
Sure you're out celebrating
Having the time of your life
I've thought of all the ways
I would come crash your party
Pop up through a mirage of balloons
Just to deflate your celebration
And flash a comfortable grin
Like I've been sitting on your couch
For more than a couple of hours
In the dark, just like stalkers do
If only I could muster up
The guts to be that crazy
Is this cream cheese frosting?
Oh, I'd love to devour
Your newfound independence
And strap it with two chains
To this chair
I'd throw away the key
Then tell you to make your greatest wish
I just want to know
Who's blowing out the candles
On your birthday cake?
Since I know it's not me

I Don't Want To

I don't want to get to know you
I didn't inquire to know
About your first dog or
How long it takes on your morning jogs
What makes you smile and cry
What makes you grateful and raise your head
To kiss the sky
I am drained and at the moment
Have nothing left to give
One-night stands might be my new thing
But who am I kidding
With my makeup, that would
Get old quickly
Plus, I don't have time
For any psycho tendencies
Why didn't you call me
Don't you really want to be with me?
It's all too much, too soon
Blue is the new red for hearts
And mine just doesn't have
Enough vitality to make room for you
It may sound cruel, but it's the truth

Good To See You

Remember that peace I talked about a few pages ago? Well, for the sake of transparency, that peace doesn't come easily. Although I had reached a new state of mind, I was still processing and dealing with thoughts of my pending divorce. If you've ever gone through a break up, then you know it's not always a simple parting of ways.

My ex-wife and I remained cordial through it all (thank God). At times, it felt like I was just going through the motions. I kept my cool during times when I was angry, confused and downright hurt. I can't speak for her, but that was at least how I felt.

One day, we met up because she had a bag of some of my things. We hadn't seen each other in a while. So, I was somewhat anxious about the meeting to say the least. We ended up talking for a long time and had an enjoyable conversation. Honestly, at some points, it felt just like old times. "What were those old times though?" I thought to myself. I felt like I was watching an outer body experience of a foreign version of myself.

My ex-wife was where she wanted to be professionally, and I was always extremely proud of her for that. She was always a natural go getter and it was one of the things that initially attracted me to her. Things seemed to be looking up for her without me in the picture. The following few days were strange. I had a feeling of disturbance and my peace was disrupted. I chalked it up to a normal reaction after not seeing her for quite some time.

There is no time table with a deadline for getting over someone you love. Since we were together for over eleven years, I always expected it to take a while for me to recover from our separation and subsequent divorce. My feelings began to take me by surprise all over again. I really disliked that sense of not being in control of my thoughts.

Acceptance is a lot easier to deal with when you're not facing a situation head on. The fact that I didn't see her for all that time, it made it easier to keep moving forward. The day that I met up with my ex-wife, I wanted to say, "What happened to us?" but I guess I didn't have the courage. Plus, my pride probably wouldn't let me say it either. It was a question I wanted answered not just from her, but also myself. Sometimes the hardest thing to accept is not being able to mend things back to the way they used to be. Once again, there was yet another hurdle to cross in processing the end of our relationship.

Shrimp And Grits

It's funny
Not in the ha-ha sense
But the ain't-this-some-ish kind of sense
Tense and uneasy
Those finite details we remember
At those low, definitive moments
I was a virgin to the preparation
Shrimp and grits
Thought I'd whip up something special
For the grand occasion
I may as well have smeared it
All over my face
Like Al Green's wife did years ago
I must admit
Those were some damn good
Shrimp and grits
Right before that WTF
Wrinkle in time of a moment arrived
Void of theatrical lines
This was real life
I scraped the scallions from
The side of the plate
In denial
As I heard familiar words
With an edgier tone
That fell on different ears
So, is this what happens
After all these years
I'm about to snap and
These piping hot
Pepper jack cheese shrimp and grits

Are about to go flying in multiple directions
Speckled across the room
See, this was a harsh lesson
To swallow and digest
That by the time the
Last candle was blown out
It was just the flicker
Of a flame that never was
Rested upon a mountain of fucking ruins
Kiss my ass
Let's please make this work
Oh my, how I've failed you
Is this how it felt those times
I acted like a jerk?
I held my head high
After all
I was not going to let
My decadent shrimp and grits
Go to waste
The same could not be said for you
You never finished your plate
It set in the fridge and soured
Just like our love
Wasting my damn good food
My damn good youthful years
I cannot transport back to the future
I cleared the table in silence
The beat of my heart thumping
Loud enough to crumble a stadium
I somehow mustered up the strength
To smile at you and see
The woman I used to know
Looking into those eyes

I saw the reflection of
The man I once was
I asked if you wanted anything else
Your reply was simply "No"
I would like to think
We both wanted what we
Could not give to each other
Just like that
There went our love
Those were some damn good
Shrimp and grits though

Let It Flood

This is so unlike me and
Out of my normal scope
I usually would have rushed to
Turn off the faucets by now
Or at the very least position my
Pots, buckets and tubs
Ever so carefully to catch the over flow
But tonight is different
I stood there
Frozen in a gaze
I watched the water rise
From the kitchen sink
As it began to quickly fill
And spill onto the counter
I did not restrict it
I did not hinder its multiple directions
Dispersed in puddles as the tiny
Waterfalls began to greet my feet with
Their sensational force
I stood there
Mesmerized as the water from the bathroom
Traveled through the soaked carpet in my bedroom
To meet me in the kitchen
And greet my ankles with a wet hello
As the levels continued to rise
I laughed at the departure of
My material things and tangible memories
That would now be mere relics
When the sun dried them all up
The neighbors began to knock at my front door
Softly at first, then pounding loudly

Hoping that I would hear them
I did
And I still stood there
Until I was ready to open the door
I waded in the water as it moved me
Me without intention or permission
After I let them bang
Until their knuckles turned raw
I swam to the front door
Turned the knob and invited them in
To join the party
They all looked at me
With perplexed expressions
That just made me enjoy the moment more
I did not apologize for getting their clothes wet
They wanted to know
And I gave them the full show
Today marked the first time
I didn't bother with the stress of
Trying to turn the faucets off
That connected to pipes
That I knew would eventually burst anyway
Today I let it flood
I rode the waves with pride and intentionality
Today I let the water lead me
Wherever it desired

Brokenness is an uninvited guest that we all must meet at some point in life.

The Dam Must Break

We are often programmed to turn off negative feelings quickly; especially men. However, there are some aspects of life that you must allow yourself to feel to heal from. This doesn't necessarily mean crying or telling your "woe is me" story to everyone you meet. I learned the importance of keeping my personal business to myself. Nevertheless, it does mean that you must acknowledge the ugly, dark corners of your deepest hurts to overcome them.

I had a choice to either be distracted or confront the certainty of my divorce head on. My job was keeping me very busy, plus my writing and publishing for other authors allowed me to sink into my own private world. I remember having a conversation with someone who didn't know what was going on with my ex-wife and I (or at least they had one hell of a poker face).

He included my ex-wife in much of the conversation and I played along like nothing ever happened. Mind you, I had stopped wearing my ring at this point. One thing I learned through this process though is that associates really didn't care about my divorce. People close to me cared, but even they had their own issues to deal with.

After that conversation (and several others like it), I realized I had to face the truth even if I put a mask up for everyone else. One of the greatest disservices you can do in life is to lie to yourself. Over time, I allowed myself to look at the old pictures. I allowed myself to get angry, smile, reminisce and yep, even cry at times. Dealing with it was not easy. I knew that if I was truly going to move on and let go of my marriage, I had to walk through the fire. I had to break down the walls and let the water come rushing in, even if it meant struggling just to stay afloat.

Running Nowhere Fast

Placing one foot in front of the other
Sweat flying off my body
As I increase in speed
I'm going to catch up to you
I'm going to run to meet us there
I'm going to travel to find me
No matter how long it takes
I imagine the seasons changing
With picturesque views of
Us on the mountain top
I don't care how much they laugh or
What they say
I'm doing this for us
I have vowed to never stop
Jumping over hurdles
Mudslides and potholes
Designed to break my stride
I look and see you lagging behind
As I ignore the doubt piercing
From your eyes
I sigh and pant for motivation
Breathing in any source of oxygen
I can find
The finish line seems so far away
Suddenly my legs and lungs are growing weary
I can't bear the strength to finish this race
When only one of us wants to stay

Pep Talk

I got this bad ass trouble maker
Weighing on my shoulder
Whispering dirty little nothings
Making my heart turn colder
I try to shut him up
But then he rears his ugly head
Telling me we can't be friends
And never talk to you again
Then I got this diplomatic peace maker
He understands that crack in the door
Is closing further with each passing day
He has hope
He is naïve and wants to believe
Only the good and won't allow
Negative energy as band aids to cope
I got these two opposing forces
Pulling me in different directions
I know which way I'm leaning
But I just want a peaceful way of being
An amicable parting free of
Confusion and disillusions

Tomorrow Will Come

I don't think I've ever been
This apprehensive about a sunrise before
When the morning comes
It will be four years since that day
Then together, now astray
Back then, boy meets world
You were my Topanga
Things were so much easier
During those days
Tomorrow will come
But girl, I can wait
It's our anniversary
Telling my boss I'm leaving early
So I can escape the remainder the day
And anticipate the day after
No roses, cards or gifts
No love like we knew it
Tell me
Do you know what to say now?

Never Again

People ask me if I ever will walk
Down that aisle again
"Hell no" is my answer
They say, "I hate to hear you say that"
So I have crafted this canned response....
Has your heart ever panged
At Christmas time
As *It's A Wonderful Life* plays?
Or during the thought of that smile
From plantains from the grocery store on Sundays?
Or finishing her sentence
Even if it's something you don't agree with
But you already know what she's about to say
Or looking away from her pretty brown eyes
Because it hurts to bad to know that
Upon their gaze
This love has dissipated
Maybe that's a little too serious
So I'll go with something a little
More trivial
Like how watermelon, honeydew melon
And anything with melon at the end of it makes her nauseous
Or how she cautiously turns up on the overpass
Sometimes with her eyes closed
Hands clenched on the steering wheel
Because the heights give her the heebie-jeebies?
No?
You cannot fathom?
Have you not had that type of encounter?
Well if so, then maybe you can understand my position

That I no longer have the energy to get
To know another woman that intricately
Just to watch the shit slip through my hands like sand
And the castle come crumbling down in the end
No thanks, I'll pass

Day In December

Crazy how that day in December
Has come full circle to this
Suspended in love's abyss
I still remember how it felt back then
Like warm honey being splashed
Underneath my skin
Lubricating my veins
My heart was limber
So naïve back then
I miss how everything was
So simple then
Now I'm wondering if
I ever should have even said it
I guess it didn't matter because
I knew that we could feel it
Without ever uttering a word
Or was I deceiving myself
Wearing rose colored glasses
In a virtual insanity
Like Jamiroquai
My eyes are bloodshot red
Watching the petals descend
As we try ever so carefully
Not to crush them
Beneath our heels
I hope this isn't how every
December is going to feel

Know This

Don't take what I'm about to say
As free reign to push my buttons
Or test the aesthetic of my heart's apparatus
Don't take this as an open invitation
To use me as the welcome door mat
You dig your shoes into
After a 12-hour day of work
And you just got caught out there
In the rain and you forgot your umbrella at home
Don't use this as collateral
To wreak havoc and irreversible damage
Or I will be forced to take back every word
And intent originally meant for good
Don't take my silence
As a nonchalant demeanor of choice
I am just taking my moment to chew
And fully digest all that has transpired
I'm not sure when I'll be done
But this much you should know
I will always love you
No matter what you do
Or wherever you go

Learn what makes your lover tick and never lose sight of it.

Out of Order

As I mentioned at the beginning, I had no intentions of writing the contents of this book. However, life and subsequently, creativity had a different plan. Tell God your plans and watch Him laugh. Throughout this entire process, I have felt like God has been laughing at some of the plans I had for my life. If I take that a step further, there were many times that I was angry at God. Honestly, I still am occasionally.

Nevertheless, my peace comes in knowing that there are no accidents in life. Choices? Yes. We all make choices in life that we must live with; no matter how sugary, bittersweet or sour they may be. Here's a bit of irony about my next book. I have two novels, *Fortune Cookie* and *No Cream in the Middle*, that are part of a trilogy series.

My ex-wife and I were talking about the third novel right before I started writing it. Suddenly, she said, "Hey, what about *When the Cookie Crumbles* for a title?" I knew I wanted the final installment of the series to have "Cookie" in the title, to symbolize an evolution and completion. Well, that was clearly in place with the title she gave me. Plus, I thought it was catchy.

I immediately loved it and told her I would likely use it if nothing else came to me. I have picked out my own titles for every other book I've written. This time was obviously very different. Another title never came and the one she chose stuck like glue.

Excerpt from *When the Cookie Crumbles*

Meanwhile, Ken picked up his phone to dial Cookie. Wait. He couldn't call her yet. He needed to wait until he got back home. Thank goodness she was out of town for work. There would have been absolutely no way he could explain coming home in the morning without letting her know of his whereabouts. Ken looked back through his text message history and saw that he did text Cookie to say goodnight shortly after 10:00 pm. Thankfully, she was hanging out with some of her coworkers and didn't text him back until a couple of hours later.

"Hello? Hey baby! The best part of waking up. Who needs Folgers, right?" Cookie smiled, still half asleep yet excited to hear her husband's voice.

"Look at you, making me blush. I just called to say good morning baby. How is the conference going so far?" Ken asked.

"Oh, it's great! I think I'm already starting to feel the struggle of getting up for two people though. Even though I haven't started to show much yet, I have a feeling this baby is not going to be a morning person. Maybe if I play my cards right, their daddy will be the designated person to make sure he or she is out of bed on time. What do you think it will be?" Cookie asked, talking a mile a minute. Her pregnancy hormones were kicking in. She was never this talkative in the morning.

Ken's heart dropped to the pit of his stomach. What was he thinking? How could he have done something so reckless, especially while Cookie was pregnant? There was an uncomfortable silence over the phone before he responded to Cookie.

About the Author

Carlos Harleaux is a native of Houston, TX, now residing near Dallas, TX. He is the founder and CEO of 7th Sign Publishing. This is his eighth literary work. His previous works include two novels (*Fortune Cookie* and *No Cream in the Middle*) and five collections of poetry (*Blurred Vision, Hindsight20/20, Honesty Box, Stingrays* and *Commissioned To Love*).

He also posts weekly blogs and enjoys helping other authors get their books published. Visit his website, www.peauxeticexpressions.com, for more information.

www.ingramcontent.com/pod-product-compliance
Lightning Source LLC
Chambersburg PA
CBHW051951290426
44110CB00015B/2197